# Wild Be

Wild Be
Copyright 2016 by One Leaf

All rights reserved. No part of this book may be used or reproduced by any means now known or to be invented without written permission of the publisher, except in the case of brief quotations used in critical articles and reviews. All inquiries should be made to:

Middle Creek Publishing & Audio
9027 Cascade Avenue
Beulah, CO 81023  USA
editor@middlecreekpublishing.com

ISBN-13: 978-0-9974200-4-3
ISBN-10: 0997420049

Cover photo & Interior Images:
One Leaf

Cover & Book Design:
David Anthony Martin, Publisher / Editor
Middle Creek Publishing & Audio

This book is dedicated to the path I have walked, the people I have hurt, the lessons I have learned, and the love that I now want to give back.

It is also dedicated to the love I am now capable of receiving. It has been a long and tough life, I have been greatly hurt in it, and I have hurt others greatly. I have reached the top of that apex, and am now able to find what it is in nature and in people that has taught me so much, and allowed me to grow, to love, and to be loved.

It is where the praise and prayer has stemmed from, originated from. I simply want to give it acknowledgement, and thanks.

# Table of Contents

| | |
|---|---|
| 8 | Being |
| 9 | Up Here |
| 11 | Brothers |
| 12 | Hymn |
| 14 | Elements |
| 15 | Roads |
| 16 | Ladders |
| 18 | Before |
| 20 | Gone Camping |
| 22 | Keep Walking |
| 23 | Mountains Speak to Me |
| 25 | Wild Speech |
| 27 | Freedom, if Ever |
| 29 | Self Confidence |
| 31 | Roots |
| 32 | One Leaf |
| 34 | Painting and Wood |
| 35 | Outhouses |
| 38 | Both |
| 40 | A Single Flower |
| 42 | Soul Fire Burning |
| 44 | Water |
| 46 | Stance |
| 48 | Montophilia |
| 50 | On the Other Hand |
| 52 | Bird in the Firebox |
| 54 | Sunday Morning Service |
| 58 | In Love With This World |
| 60 | Delicious is the Day |

| | |
|---|---|
| 62 | My Grandmother Painted |
| 66 | Charge Yet to Heed |
| 68 | Pony Up |
| 70 | I Love You in Yellow |
| 72 | Horizons Never Lie |
| 74 | Winds |
| 76 | Growth Rings |
| 78 | The Art of You |
| 80 | Gratitude & Abundance |
| 82 | Walk Into Me |
| 86 | All the Way |

# Wild Be

One Leaf

Middle Creek Publishing & Audio
2016  Beulah, CO

#cosmic #choices #tobeornottobe #thatisthequestion #ornot #oneleaf

## Being

Living is tough,
no doubt.

I sometimes see myself
and feel
bruised in blues,
a cloudy dramatic and shady sky,

a sky that takes no prisoners
and offers no freedoms,

a sky that allows the choice
to be yours and yours alone,

the same choice we all face
everyday in our own personal mirrors,

the choice of acknowledging
that we are cosmic beings
worthy of the choice

of simply being.

Wild be.

## Up Here

Up here,
we sometimes live above
the clouds,
sometimes in
the clouds,
sometimes below
the clouds.

But we never look at each other
and ask each other
how we do it.

No.

We simply give each other
that knowing look
as if we share and indulge in
the secrets of each other;

we bond with one another
through our unspoken,
yet definitive energy
of connection
to one another;

we pray
one to the other
in a sort of communal dialogue
which allows us to deepen
the extended family roots of ourselves
one to the other.

We will always be here
for each other,
we will always be here
just like our Mother,

the Earth.

Wild be.

# Brothers

I said to him
in Raven talk
that I admired him,

and loved him like a brother.

He, in turn, asked
if I was cold without any feathers,

to which I said
no, brother, I'm not,

but I really don't think
that he believed me.

Wild be.

# Hymn

Congregates, again,
please open your hymnals
to pages earth and sky.

We will now sing the songs
taught to us by
and in praise of
our mother and father.

Let the breath of the most deep
permeate your lungs
and charge your words,

let the soil and stone of the most solid
permeate your bones
and solidify your convictions

as you become the songbirds
of your intentions.

I sing unto you
as you sing amongst
your brethren

that we are all the living bridge
of the morning time

that through our breath at the head
and through our rootedness
at the feet

we are the ones that connect the two
and where the most profound hearts beat.

Wild be.

#nature #elements #good #morning #always #all #ways #oneleaf

# Elements

Another shot
of the Four Elements
as I see them:

earth, air, fire, and water.

Nature does not skirt around us,
we skirt around Nature.

Wild be.

# Roads

How does one
know the difference between
a road that leads somewhere
and a road that goes nowhere?

The answer is that
there is no difference
between roads themselves.

Every road is both.

The difference is found
only within the heart
of the traveler him or herself:

in their open-mindedness
in their powers of observation
in their attitude and perceptions

in their ability to believe
that whatever they want to make possible
is indeed their manifest
reality.

Wild be.

## Ladders

I've climbed many a ladder
in my life,
and in order to remain humble
I've climbed back down to the bottom
of each and every one of them.
Even if the top
reaches for the sky,
and there is no limit to that sky,

the bottom is resting on the earth,
a solid earth,
the one that holds the roots
to every blade of grass
the same as it does
for every living
breathing being.

I for one am a climber,
but I am also a thread
of the earth's grit and fiber.

Wild be.

#ghosts #oneleaf

# Before

Driving around
these old and ghostly mountains
makes me, too,
feel as if I was here before

before power lines and roads
before trees and wind and rain
before the things I've never known
before I truly became me.

Wild be.

#blackandwhite #camping #comanche #quanahparker #good #evening #always #all #ways #oneleaf

## Gone Camping

I'm going camping
in the Comanche Peak Wilderness
outside of Ft. Collins, CO
this weekend,

named after the esteemed
Tribe of the Comanche People,
which dawned
the stunning man and leader
known as Quanah Parker,
the last Chief of the Comanche Indians.

The world sure has changed a lot
since then,,
and I wouldn't even be surprised
if the moonrise and the sunset
were also in different places.

Our world
seems quite a bit more black and white
than theirs did
I would say,

which is why we camp
in the first place,
I would also say,

for the benefit of removing ourselves,
if only temporarily,
from the ho hum,
to get out into the colorful unknown,
to feel a little bit more of the A-ho.

I don't know,
I'm sure we all go

into the woods
into the wild
into the nature
into the child

of who we were
before being conditioned
by our own conditioning,

for different reasons.

But I would also venture out
into the wooded untamed
to say that we probably have
more reasons the same
for why we go camping
than we do reasons that are different.

The bottom line,
which does happen to be
black and white,

is that I don't care why
I go camping,
I just care that I do
go camping.

Wild be.

# Keep Walking

I've walked my path
the only and the best
way that I know how.

I've asked countless questions
along the way,

I've examined myself
openly and honestly,

I've bowed down to the greater spirit
on high
and asked for guidance,

I've made my mistakes
and taken ownership of them,

I've looked at you in my mind's eye
and forgiven you,

I've looked in my own eyes
and forgiven me too.

The only other thing I know to do
is to keep on walking
toward peace and tranquility.

Wild be.

# Mountains Speak To Me

Mountains speak to me
in consonants and verbs
as if they don't have the patience
for subtle lines of poetry
that fall softly on your ear,
even though I know
mountains have all the patience
in the world.

Water and clouds speak to me
in vowels and adjectives,
as if they have way too much to say
for mere poetry,
as if prose is a vice
they simply cannot escape,
nor do they want to,

yet I see them,

I see them move
in every direction but backwards,
as if movement has been
the only thing they've ever known,
because it is.

If I were the book
in the hands and minds
of every living reading soul alive,

I would articulate to them
through my printed letters
that we are all beings
of the deepest width and breadth,

that we need both,
the poetry and the prose,

that either way and both,
we simply need our truths
to be spoken.

Wild be.

# Wild Speech

Some believe
that by speaking to a wild animal
in an indigenous or aboriginal language,
unlike and rather than
any civilized language,
the animal will actually turn
to receive the communication
and gesture of friendliness
by looking at you directly in the eye.

And when they do this,
it is their way of acknowledging
an understanding
between the two of you
of brotherhood and peace,
that we are both here as equals
to share fairly and respectfully
the bounties of this round earth
that are here for the both of us.

So I said unto him:

*Hah-tee-toh,*
*wessah kee-nah-la nee chey-nee-nah,*
*nee-yah-weh mich-toh*
*wessah chobeka.*

*Sa-la-no-kee.*

In turn the coyote said unto me:

*You are welcome, my brother,*
*and thank you for the same.*

He went his way
and I went mine,
and the only other sound
was the howling of time.

Wild be.

# Freedom, If Ever

If there was ever a mountain top
we wanted to get to
but couldn't,

it wasn't because they weren't there
and ours for the taking.

If ever there was a darkened cloud
that did not intimidate us,

it was not because we didn't know
and have faith in the fact that
sunshine was flowing just above
and beyond the thing
and would be there soon.

And if ever there were
fields and plains of buffalo grass
that did not get laid down upon
by us and the fullness of our own bodies,

it certainly was not because
we were unaware
of our relationship
of our dependency
of our own desperation
and utter love for the earth itself.

There's an ancestry to the land
and we are the ancestors.

There's a freedom to its geography,

but we each have to allow
ourselves to be free.

Wild be.

## Self Confidence

Admittedly,
I've been too big for my britches
more than once;

I've looked at myself
like I was God's gift to creation
at least a dozen times;

and I've drilled my opinions
and attitudes and judgments
into the world
as if the world itself
was just begging to learn
the personal brand of knowledge
that I had, that I invented,
and that only I could provide.

But I've been wrong
more times than right,

and I honestly strip down
to nothing more than bones
just like the rest of us.

And my soul,
even though I hope it lives forever,
has no more importance
than a sun or a sky
or a great idea.

These realizations though,
do not prevent me
from holding my chin up high,
sticking my chest out,

and holding the calloused hand
that I am the owner of
directly on top of every single well
I have ever dug.

I will forever stand in confidence,
whether right or wrong,
at everything I've ever done,
for some things simply
cannot be denied:

I am still the owner
of my own reality,
whatever that means.


Wild be.

# Roots

It's believed, scientifically,
that Aspen trees
are the largest
single living organism
on earth
because of the way their roots
are all connected together.

Which leads me to believe
that humanity
is actually the largest
single living organism
on earth
because of the way our roots
are all connected together.

I can't speak for you,
but I really mean it when I say
"All my relations."

Wild be.

# One Leaf

One of many
Trees of Life

The trunk is the core,
the main embodiment
of all Life.

The roots are how we
are connected to,
grounded through,
fed by,
and integral with
the Earth itself.

The reaching branches,
all the different cultures,
all the different races,
all the different everything
of all of Humanity.

The leaves
are the individual people.

One leaf,
me.

Wild be.

#tree #wood #painting #dreamcatcher #oneleaf

## Painting and Wood

Sometimes I don't think
the differences between wood
and a painting
are all that distinct.

I see wild shapes in both their forms,
and lots of texture
in both their barks.

There is a movement
in each of them
that not even the slowest of songs
could slow down,
let alone stop.

They are both made
by a creator,
by a nature,
and each of their meanings
is beheld by the beholder.

I revere them both the same,
the painting and the tree,
equally.

Wild be.

# Outhouses

It's amazing
the kinds and numbers of outhouses
I've made over the years.

For 17 years
and through the raising
of two children
we lived without any running water,

certainly no hot water
or bathing facilities,
no flush toilet at all,
and no super strong desire
to have them anyway.

I've dug holes out in the open,
made crude pine branch shelters,
built tiny A-frames
out of scrap plywood
and rusty tin,
used composting toilets
and humanure systems,
repurposed little closets like this one,
and even had the luxury outhouse
of all time,

with salvaged redwood floors,
insulated and painted walls
with pictures hanging on them,
topped off with a real roof
and a solar light.

Then I built a "real" house,
as the flatlanders might say.

Now I have sinks galore
with hot and cold running water,
three flush toilets
without hot water,
and three whole showers,
count 'em,
three.

People like to say I'm lucky.
I like to say I'm clean.

Wild be.

#zhuangzi #dreamon #butterfly #man #eveningisaboy #good #evening #always #all #ways #oneleaf

# Both

I came upon the fence post
of the evening time,
when critters were slowing down
and birds were resting their wings.

I leaned on it softly
to ponder,
when the thought occurred to me:

"I do not know
whether I was then a man dreaming
I was a butterfly,

or whether I am now
a butterfly
dreaming I am a man."

And after watching the clouds
shift and change
I came to the conclusion
that I am both,

both butterfly and man,

strong and delicate alike
and at the same time.

And what really
is the most important
is not the defining of my essential being,
but rather,
the simple act
of continuous dreaming.

Wild be.

#good #evening #always #all #ways #oneflower #oneleaf

# A Single Flower

A single flower
has fields of glorious beauty in it
just oozing out and leaking
off its every petal and stamen.

I know
because I've lain under them
before,
imitating those petals
with my tongue,
hoping for the living drops
to drop on it.

I've sung the songs of the stamens,
each and every one of them,
until the sound waves behaved
like fields and waves of grass
being danced to the wind.

I'm a friend to this flower
as I am a friend to you,

and as obvious as it is
that the sun is yellow,
it's just as obvious
that the sky is blue.

Wild be.

#soul #fire #burning #poem #four #elements #earthcentered #poetry #poetsofinstagram #writersofinstagram #oneleaf #wildbe

# Soul Fire Burning

Tell me that you cannot feel the grit of the earth itself on your own original hands and between your five fingers, or that its purely rustic and cavernous smell has not encrusted the insides of your dutiful nostril, and I will tell you

your soul fire's not burning.

Tell me that the sun lives not in your heart, but in the sky alone, that you are not empassioned by its influence at all, that you would not die to love someone, and that someone would not die to love you, and I will tell you

your soul fire's not burning.

Tell me that your own body is not made of water, that its contoured and rhythmic movements are not exactly like any other fluid river or ocean that has ever existed, has ever crested and fallen with the daily moon, and I will tell you

your soul fire's not burning.

Tell me that the unlimited skies cannot be found right there in your eyes, that clouds themselves cannot be found in your personal lungs, or that your very breath doesn't affect wind currents on a global scale, and I will tell you

your soul fire's not burning.

But go look at yourself in the mirror, stare directly into your eyes and see what I see, because there's no doubt about it, you absolutely do have a stunning

soul fire burning.

#water #wisdom #bluelake #indianpeakswilderness #continentaldivide #oneleaf

Water

I've been wanting to write about water for some reason not sure why. So I went to Blue Lake today, to play with a poem or three.

There is nothing more fascinating to me than being up on the Divide and thinking about water:

how it can land on one side or the other, East or West. It's either going to pass through Oklahoma and the land of the red earth or through the Grand Canyon's jaggedly deep and brown land.

I could literally pour half my water bottle on one side of the Divide and half on the other in order to prove those pursuits.

But water fallen on this side is not any better, not one single drop, than water fallen on the other side. It's just a matter of course and luck of the drop.

To say that eastern water is better than western water would be like saying that humans also have different values on different sides of imaginary lines.

The fact is they do not.

All water, like humans, no matter which direction it flows, is of equal value, equal quench, equal beautiful, equal everything.

How could a cloud be more valuable than a lake, or rain more valuable than the sea? A river should be no more relevant than a tear, the way I see it, since water makes up most of me.

Wild be.

#goodevening #oneleaf

## Stance

Stand alone

if you have to.

Root yourself in the earth,
any earth,
whatever it takes.

Rocks may act
like they have no give,
but they do.

They give.

And so should we.

Wild be.

#goodnight #mountains #oneleaf

# Montophilia

It's not enough
to just see them from a distance,

I need to see them
to feel them
to touch them
to taste them,

from deep within.

I've always been
truly in love
with the mountains.

Wild be.

#goodmorning #inside #hidden #secret #love #oneleaf

# On The Other Hand

On the other hand,
I am also totally fascinated
with the evolutionary growing process
of all the plants
growing here in the desert.

Nearly every single one of them
says to you loud and clear

"Do not,
and I mean without a doubt,
absolutely,
without question,
plain and simple,
with no two ways about it,

do not touch me."

Why, I wonder.

Who and what
are they protecting
themselves from?

Why was, and is, it so imperative
that they be left
so alone?

Is there gold inside of them?
Is there water?
Is there a valuable life lesson
for why I can't find her?

Whatever it is
I'm sure it has to be earned.

Whatever it is,
I bet you anything,
I just know it has to do
with love.

Wild be.

#set #love #free #setlovefree #bird #woodstove #ash #trapped #chimneysweep #pobrecitio #neighborhoodchimneysweep #goldhillcolorado #unexpected #surprise #rescue #oneleaf

# Bird in the Firebox

Good Evening!

Went to do a chimney sweep
in Gold Hill today

and after opening the stove door
to inspect the inside of the firebox

I found this little guy in there
buried in the ash and pitch dark.

Pobrecito!

He flew out in a major cloud of dust
and I managed to catch him
in a bright and sunny square window.

The word in Shawnee for little bird
sounds like *"whiskey-low-thah-kee,"*

so I said:

*"Hah-tee-toh whiskey-low-thah-kee nee-cheh-nee-nah.
Nee-yah-weh mich-toe wessah chobeka."*

And the little bird said back to me:

*"Bezon nee-cheh-nee-nah.
Wessah kee-nah-la nee-yah-weh."*

Then I opened my hand
the same as I would open my heart
and it flew away.

We had not really
anymore to say.

Wild be.

#sunday #morning #sermon #love #forgiveness #equals #same #sing#songs #oneleaf

# Sunday Morning Sermon

Good Sunday Morning!

Dear fellow sisters and brothers and children
of the Universe,

Dear circular participants
in this loving and forgiving life we call Life,

Dear judgemental beings
trying so diligently, and so desirous of being,
nonjudgemental,

Dear all living and breathing creatures
with and without impeccable tongues
and enlightened hearts,


please,


before we sing our songs
of gratitude and mountainous joys,

before we open our hymnals
to the book of humanity,

before we relish in rejoicing
like eating dessert before the feast,

let us look each other in the eyes
and let us look, each one of us, in the I,
and let us pray.

Let us pray to the source from whence we came.

Let us pray to the presence,
for it is a present, of this very day.

Let us pray for tomorrow,
and let us lead, ourselves, the way.

It will be under the direction and ambition
of our own very choices
that we choose to raise ourselves upon high
with our own morning suns.

It will be through our own chosen perseverance
that we follow the course of the light,
from south to north,
from east to west,
through any and every trial and tribulation
of the great long day.

And it will be us and ourselves and only those
who will be able to take responsibility or not
for their heavenly and celestial views
of the stars and the moons
within the vastness of space
after the long day of trudging
that it took us to get there.

Oh yes,


let us pray the concept and idea and reality
of humanity
has not been lost
upon our own and selfish desires.


Oh please,


let us care one for the other
as if there is no difference,
as if there is no separation,
as if there is no individuality and independence
between us.

Oh Love and Forgiveness,
You are the Blessed and Singular One
that we are all striving for.

May we be you and you be us,
may you help us live a life that's just.

Now let us sing.

Wild be.

#world #all #around #us #natural #love #goodnight #oneleaf

# In Love with this World

Good, oh so very good, evening!

I just have to say,
whether it be through the tip of my tongue
or through the tip of my finger,

that I am in love with this world
and everything around me
in it.

There is not a shadow-bellied cloud,
an unequally leveled foothill,
an unshaven and wild meadow,
or a single tree out of plumb

that does not suit my fancy
in every single way
that I know how to define the word
fancy.

I cannot imagine the slightest wind blown
or a single raindrop thrown
that does not honor me to the fullest
by laying itself down upon me,
even when I have other expectations.

The world does not do right or wrong,
the world just does.

The world does not make decisions,
the world simply makes us.

The world does not judge,
the world judges not.

The world does not love us,
the world is only love.

The world is not below us,
the world is all around.

I am the world
and the world am I,

our love for it comes natural,
we shouldn't have to try.
Wild be.

# Delicious is the Day

Good Evening!

Delicious is the day
that tastes like yellow leaves,
that feels like luscious breeze,
that makes me want to play
inside your wildest dreams,

and leads me to the words that say
nothing more than

I love you.

Wild be.

#delicious #yellow #dreams #oneleaf

#poor #artist #art #paint #painting #earth #grandmother #love #unstoppable #spirit #conduit #oneleaf

# My Grandmother Painted

Good Evening!

My Grandmother lived nearly her whole life
either in or near
the White Oak Hills of Oklahoma,

which was the end of The Trail of Tears
for the Shawnee People.

When she was a young child
her parents raised her and her siblings
on their one acre
of Indian allotment land.

They were poor.

They grew everything they could,
or was possible,
in that red terra cotta land,
and everything else they either bought
in a 50 lb. bag or they traded and bartered for.

But my grandmother was always hungry
for a lot more than food.

Even as a four year old, she was a painter
and she knew it.

One time her parents returned home
to find that she had painted the dog,
the white family dog,
yellow,
with a bottle of mustard,

and she died nearly 90 years later
with yellow still being her favorite color.

She was a painter
and she could not be stopped.

One might not think that the land,
especially that one Indian acre,
could grow oil paints, or acrylic paints,
or any kind of paints at all really,
particularly the kind of paints that came
in those fancy neat little tubes with lids.

And one might not think that the land
could provide brushes and canvasses and easels,
or any kind of cleaning agents, for that matter,

and in their way of thinking
they might've been right.

But my grandmother was not an overthinker,
she was a doer.

She crushed up every different colored rock
she could find,

she scooped up bowls of mud
in every tint you could imagine,

she collected clouds in her hands
and fire soot on her fingers,

and let me tell you,
she painted.

She painted with fingers, cloths, sticks, leaves,
pebbles and stones, feathers, strings,
salvaged pieces of junk metal,
and anything else she could get her hands on.

By God she painted.

And in the beginning,
she had nothing but the earth itself

on that little Indian acre,
creative ingenuity and pure desire
with which to make it happen.

But in time,
she painted her way through the ownership
of at least 5 of her own art galleries

in every kind of medium,
in every type of format,
in every style of genre,
with every kind of paint,
on every surface imaginable.

Yes, my grandmother was a conduit of Spirit,
and the spirit of her work proves that she meant it.

Wild be.

#rhythm #flow #whitewater #rapids #river #life
#metaphor #charge #heed #oneleaf

## A Charge Yet to Heed

Good evening!

My life is a river
and I'm either along for the ride,
or I'm not.

I'm also no longer fooled by the straightness
of singular sections of the river, either,
cause the rest of it ain't straight
by any means,

and I know it.

Fighting it would be death,
arguing it would be torture,
resisting it would be neverending,

and talking it down like a poet
would result in me running out of words to say
and orders to put them in,

which would be like death all over again.

I'll go along for the ride,
but not because I don't have a choice to make
in the matter.

I do.

I choose to ride.
I choose to flow.
I choose to give-in to gravity

like it's my lover,
like it's my my downright pride and joy.

I've seen other people defy
the white-watered raging and turbulent rapids.

And other people have seen me defy.

We give to each other
the strength that we need

to love and keep loving,
to charge yet to heed.

Wild be.

## Pony Up

Good Morning!

Well the weekend has done fallen apart
like a crusty old and splintered wagon
from back in the day,

and all I can do
is jump on my pony direct
and charge ahead into Monday.

I'll see you out there, on the trail,
or at least I hope to,
where the grass grows high
upon the bend of our horizons.

No need to be lookin' for me
or awaitin' mine arrival,
just know I'm already out there
workin' hard at keepin' my heart full.

Wild be.

#monday #morning #full #heart #working #hard #tall #grass #horizon
#broken #wagon #oneleaf

#pure #yellow #wildflower #buzzing #bumblebee #sublime #nectar #love #oneleaf

## I Love You in Yellow

Good Evening.

I love you in yellow.

I love that you are the whole,
as well as all the individual parts.

I love that you are many micro flowers
making up the single flower.

I love yellow next to me,
and how it goes so well with my blue eyes.

I love that I see a sprinkling of snow
within your yellow.

I love that I can see other worlds,
other earths,
other universes,
within the core and center of your yellow.

I love that you have reaching
and radiating and petaly arms
like a big and round and yellow sun.

I love that you have a yellow scent,
a wonderful and yellowy scent
that I want to smell and breathe in deeply,

that holds within its character
the entirety and expansive breadth
of an entire Spring.

I love that you attract bees
with your sweetly sublime and sugary nectar,

and that I must be part bee.

I love that we are wild together,
and really can't get enough
of all that forever has to offer.

I'd love to taste your yellow.

I love the yellow in you
because it brings out the yellow in me,

and I'm flying around in circles
buzzing like a bumble bee.

I love you in yellow.

Wild bee.

# Horizon's Never Lie

Good Evening Darling.

The thought of your curves
like rounded edges of water
not only makes me thirsty,
but makes my heart beat faster.

The vision of your clouds
billowing all around me,
like the spark in your eye,
electric yellow candy.

There's a line between wet and dry
that I really want to walk with you,
that I truly want to cusp with you,
that I really and truly want to bridge

with you.

I would love it if we could lay like land
to the point where we touch the sky
and ask every question under the sun
because horizons never lie.

Wild be.

#horizons #never #lie #oneleaf

#wind #seasons #phases #leaves #life #poets #air #powerful #meaningful #thankful #oneleaf

# Winds

Good Morning!

I've sat in the springtime and waited
for the Aspens to sprout buds,
and then to leaf,
just so I could hear
the very first wind of the season
blow through them,
to make that sound
that only Aspen leaves can make
when the wind makes them dance and quiver
and shake themselves against each other.

I've stood among the warm outside
of a calm and late summertime afternoon
and noticed
how the warm and lower elevation temperatures
start climbing the mountains,

and how the colder higher elevation temperatures
race themselves downward
creating wind as they trade places,

and I've been in awe.

I've sat myself down under the charming grove,
in the cooler throes of autumn,
and watched every single minute
as a leaf turns from green to yellow,

and then I've laid myself down upon my back,
face up,
and waited for the wind
to blow them off their branches

so they could float their pretty little selves right on down
to me, only to me, all the way over me, me me me,

like I alone was the earth
they were meant to cover,

until I could gently and softly fall asleep,
my windy blanket of leaves
protecting me.

And I've listened to the wind screech and howl,
and watched as it felled trees
during the brutal cutting of wintertime,
when the wind has teeth
and a lot to say,
and the last thing you want to do
is to interrupt it.

Oh yes, the wind and I, we are friends,
two poets who simply have too much to speak about,
too much built up inside of us,
who need to let it out,
all of it,
out.

So this is where I'll pause,
for I need to catch my breath,
for I need to breathe in deeply,
for I need to simply be.

Wild be.

# Growth Rings

Best of Evenings!
I want to walk with you somewhere,
I want to walk with you anywhere.

We can follow a path
or we can make our own,
just as long as we go
somewhere that lasts.

I'm not looking for seasonal
or beautiful but shallow
undergrowth.

I'm looking for the innumerable
growth rings
that encircles the strength
of our love.

Wild be.

#innumerable #love #growth #rings
#walkwithme #oneleaf

#priceless #art #collector #invaluable #painting #oneleaf

# The Art of You

Good Morning!

If I could paint you
I would paint you with grass.

I might just flip the trees over, too,
and use them like brushes
to paint you with strokes that have never been stroked,

like butterfly kisses
in the small of your back.

The paint would be painted
so thickly laid,

it would have to be,

for it would need to be textured
like landscape
like overly scenic views,
like feathery clouds and branches,

like you.

I would lay you down like sky,
paint so silky smooth and baby blue
that I would have to use clouds

in order to dab you with shade
in order to shade you with shadow
in order to shadow your depths,
to bring life to your color.

Oh I can just see it now!

A painting of you so grand
that even my grandmother would be proud,
and she is not easy to please!

I can hear her now
saying how there is not too much,
but just the perfect amount

of that mountain showing,
of that hillside sloping,
of pointing tall and piney trees,
of aspens and their leaves still growing.

She would even point out
that those juniper bushes in June
have never been so well-laid,

and that she can tell
their odor was certainly a lot more pungent
in April than it was in May.

Yes, my senses would come alive
through painting, my painting, of you,

and no, I'll never stop
reveling in the art of you.

Wild be.

# Gratitude & Abundance

Good Morning!

Another word for Gratitude
is Abundance.

When you give thanks,
when you are grateful,
when you say thank you

for all the things you have
and don't have,

you are saying
that you want it to come back to you
full circle round.

And manifestation
is nothing more than intention.

If you lack it,
intend on having it.

If you want it,
thank it.

If you have it,
love it.

Be grateful
to be abundant.

Wild be.

#gratitude #abundance #give #thanks #gift #love
#manifest #intention #oneleaf

#walk #into #me #foreverly #oneleaf

## Walk Into Me

Good Morning!

I have walked
over many a parts of this land.

I have seen skyscapes pass by overhead
that have made me feel
as if the world was coming to an end
every bit as much as they made me feel
that the world was just being born again,

right here,
right now,
today,
all the time,

over and over and over again,

and I always wanted to feel
that very same way.

I've laid my heart down
and practically buried it
right there in the righteous ground,
under mountains,

and I've also filled my heart up with the stuff,

literally shovels and wheel barrows worth
of the earth
have I poured into my heart
in order to give it something to beat about.

Oh Darlin', walking these hills,
for us,
will be like walking right into the heart and soul
of our very beings together,

like walking into every single sight and sound
that I've ever dreamed of
and imagined looking at
and listening to
with you,

like walking right into the center of the song

that if ever I sang,
I was singing to you,

that if ever you sang,
you were singing to me,

that if ever we loved,
you and me,

it was today and forward,
foreverly.

Wild be.

# Postscript

#visionquest #hike #explore #delve #ask #listen #numberone #numerouno #start #with #yourself #pebble #water #rings #ripple #effect #growth #gratitude #oneleaf

# All the Way

People Good Morning!

I am not,
you are not,
we are not

reflective examples, individually,
of all these crazy things
we see in the world
going on around us.

Yes,
it is our job to investigate,
it is our job to think critically,
it is our job to question,
it is our job to vote,
it is our job to ask
the invisible and higher
powers that be
for help and for guidance,

and yes,

it is our job then to listen,
and to come up with our own conclusions
that sit right within our own hearts
and minds and consciousness,

but then,
after all of that,

is it then our right to judge,
is it then helpful to rant and rave,
is it then powerful and poignant

to point and blame,

I think not.

If it is not apparent to you
what it is that you can do

to be of service,
to be of help,
to be of non-condonement,
to be of non-acceptance,

basically, to be of love,

then perhaps it is time
for you to go deeper within your self
and ask your own heart.

Perhaps it is now the time
to Cry for a Vision.

In order for us to help the world,
it is essential for us
to start most significantly
with our own selves.

We must know

WHO we are,
WHAT we are,
WHERE we are,
WHEN we are,
WHY we are,

and HOW we are.

Walk the hills and recesses

within your own mind and self.

Explore and discover and ask.

Open yourself to the answers
that your inner powers will offer you
if you simply and humbly and honestly
are willing to ask the questions.

The world needs us, for sure,
but more importantly than that,
the world needs you
to be all the way you.

Wild be

## About the Author

One Leaf is an artist, a professional straw-bale and green builder, a craftsman, a multi-business owner, and a poet.

He lives at the elevation of 9,200 feet in a 100% off-the-grid, straw-bale home he built in the forest near the small mountain town and anarchic community of Ward, CO.

This is his first collection of poetry, but certainly isn't his last.

# Middle Creek Publishing Titles

## Non-Fiction

Lessons from Fighting The Black Snake at Standing Rock
by Nick Jaina & Leslie Orihel
Photographs my Taylor Ross

## FICTION

Messiah Complex and Other Stories
by Michael Olin-Hitt
Winner of the 2015 Osprey Fiction Award

## POETRY

Wild Be
by One Leaf

Cirque & Sky
by Kathleen Willard
Winner of the 2015 Fledge Poetry Chapbook Award

Phases
by Erika Moss Gordon
Winner of the 2015 Fledge Poetry Chapbook Award

Deepening the Map
by David Anthony Martin

Span
by David Anthony Martin
An all-Colorado ECOCO Book

www.ingramcontent.com/pod-product-compliance
Lightning Source LLC
Chambersburg PA
CBHW042338150426
43195CB00001B/29